My FUTURE CAREER

Working in the
Food Industry

Margaret McAlpine

GARETH**STEVENS**
PUBLISHING
A WRC Media Company

Please visit our web site at: **www.garethstevens.com**
For a free color catalog describing Gareth Stevens Publishing's
list of high-quality books and multimedia programs, call
1-800-542-2595 (USA) or 1-800-387-3178 (Canada).
Gareth Stevens Publishing's fax: (414) 332-3567.

Library of Congress Cataloging-in-Publication Data

McAlpine, Margaret.
    Working in the food industry / Margaret McAlpine.
       p. cm. — (My future career)
    Includes bibliographical references and index.
    ISBN 0-8368-4776-8 (lib. bdg.)
    1. Food service—Vocational guidance—Juvenile literature.
  2. Food industry and trade—Vocational guidance—Juvenile literature.
  I. Title. II. Series.
  TX911.3.V62M39   2005
  647.95'023—dc22   2005042457

This edition first published in 2006 by
Gareth Stevens Publishing
A WRC Media Company
330 West Olive Street, Suite 100
Milwaukee, Wisconsin 53212 USA

Editor: Dorothy L. Gibbs
Inside design: Peta Morey
Cover design: Melissa Valuch

Picture Credits
Angela Hampton Family Life Picture Library 30, 32. **APM Studios:** Andrew Parris
15, 26, 27, 37, 39, 40, 41, 57, 59 (bottom). **Chapel Studios:** Zul 51. **Corbis:**
Roger Ball 46; Paul Barton 25; Dave Bartruff 19 (top); Leland Bobbé 59 (top);
Philippe Caron 13; Christopher Cormack 14; Dex Images 52; Macduff Everton 20;
Jon Feingersh 4, 9; Lois Ellen Frank 11 (left), 29; Owen Franken 49; Charles Gold
42; John Henley 54; Jose Luis Pelaez, Inc. 7, 11 (right); Helen King 16, 19 (bottom);
Robert Levin 5; John Madere 47; Laureen March 28; Don Mason 53; Roy Morsch
22; Charles O'Rear 38; Gregory Pace 24; Andre Perlstein 17; Mark Peterson 6, 8;
Reuters 43; Pete Saloutos 50; Chuck Savage 44, 56; Tom Stewart 31, 35; David
Thomas/PictureArts 36; Randy M. Ury 21; Peter Vadnal 45; Jeff Zaruba 55. **Corbis
Sygma:** Eric Robert 12. **Getty Images:** cover. Mediscan 34. **Science Photo
Library:** Maximilian Stock, Ltd. 48; TEK Image 23. **Topham:** Journal-Courier/The
ImageWorks 33. **Note:** Photographs illustrating "A day in the life of . . ." pages are
posed by models.

Gareth Stevens Publishing thanks the following individuals and organizations for
their professional assistance: Donna Glassman, Chef and Owner, Herbs and Spice,
LLC Catering; Sam Metcalfe, Seven Dials restaurant; Kathy Kiely-Bohlman, Brands
Manager, Reinhart Chef; Terese Allen, food writer and cookbook author based in
Madison, WI; Elizabeth Jackelen, RD, CD, Owner and Consultant Dietitian, Midwest
Dietitians, LLC; Robert H. Hagen, Photographer, Reiman Media; and Jack Kaestner,
Executive Chef and Chef Member of the Research Chefs Association.

Contents

Words that appear in the text in **bold**
type are defined in the glossary.

Caterer

What is a caterer?

Caterers plan, prepare, and serve food for banquets, business meetings, conferences, and weddings, as well as for many other kinds of meetings, parties, and celebrations, including events held in private homes. When it comes to menu planning and food preparation, caterers provide a professional touch.

A caterer's special touch often includes table settings and decorations as well as food preparation.

Caterers may be hired to cook for just a few people or for hundreds of people. Unlike a cook or a chef, however, a caterer usually prepares food for an event in his or her own kitchen, then takes the food wherever the customer wants to have it served. The final steps of food preparation, which typically include assembling, arranging, and **garnishing** the food, are usually completed at the event location. Some customers want caterers to deliver the food, then leave the event, but, more often, caterers stay to serve the food and clean up afterwards.

A Special Cake for a Special Day

Serving cake has long been a wedding tradition. Today, wedding cakes are made in a variety of styles and flavors — traditional white, rich chocolate, fruitcake, cheesecake, or even ice-cream cake — and they are almost always large. At the wedding of Britain's Queen Victoria and Prince Albert, in 1840, the cake was 9 feet (3 meters) across and weighed about 300 pounds (136 kilograms).

Caterers are specialists in preparing large quantities of food for large groups of people, which is why businesses hire them for conferences and annual meetings. Some businesses even have caterers working for them on a regular basis. The various airlines, for example, use catering companies to provide prepared meals that can be heated up by flight attendants during the journey.

Many caterers are self-employed, which means they work for themselves and have to find their own clients and keep their own accounts. Some caterers maintain a staff of employees, others hire help, as needed, to prepare food, transport it, set it out, or serve it.

A wedding is usually a catered event, with food served as either a **buffet** or a sitdown meal. The caterer may also be asked to provide the wedding cake.

Main responsibilities of a caterer

Companies, organizations, and private individuals hire caterers to plan, calculate costs, and prepare and deliver food for their events. Carrying out these responsibilities usually starts with a meeting at which the caterer and the customer discuss the details of the event. Necessary information for a caterer includes:

Most catering jobs are team efforts. Even with a lot of help, however, the work can be fast-paced and hectic.

- the date and time of the event
- where the event will be held
- the purpose of the event
- the type of catering services needed
- a description of the **venue**'s dining area and any kitchen facilities that are available (Hot foods require stoves or ovens and cold foods need to be stored in refrigerators.)

Good Points and Bad Points

"Getting compliments from my customers about how much they enjoyed my food is very satisfying. It's nice to feel that I've helped make someone's wedding or special celebration a success."

"Sometimes, I can't get the ingredients I need, or one of my staff calls in sick at the last minute. When things go wrong, my job is stressful. I can't afford to let customers down or spoil anyone's special day."

To help a customer decide what to serve at an event a caterer will:

- make general suggestions and ask about the customer's food preferences and budget guidelines
- draw up sample menus with approximate costs, taking into account the amount of money the customer has to spend and the kitchen and dining facilities available for the event

Beyond making foods look good and taste good, caterers must meet strict laws and standards for health and cleanliness.

After a menu has been decided, the caterer will:

- calculate the total cost of the job and prepare a **contract** for the customer to sign
- purchase ingredients
- coordinate all food preparation, cooking, and storage that can be done before the event

On the day of the event, the caterer will:

- complete any menu items that need last-minute preparation
- deliver the food
- set up buffet service or serve the food to guests, depending on the terms of the catering contract
- clear away dishes and leftovers, making sure that kitchen and dining areas are left spotlessly clean

Main qualifications of a caterer

Food knowledge and cooking skills

As almost anyone can guess, caterers have to be good cooks, but their **culinary** abilities must go beyond just cooking. Caterers must know about all kinds of foods, keep track of food trends, have good senses of taste and smell, and be able to create and modify recipes and produce a wide range of attractively presented dishes, meals, and menus.

Caterers who are responsible for serving the food and drink at an event must be sure their staff is properly trained and has clear instructions.

Business skills

Owning or operating a catering company calls for a wide range of business skills. Besides planning and cooking, caterers also have to negotiate loans, set up company accounts, deal with suppliers, attract customers, draw up contracts, and keep detailed records.

Math and bookkeeping abilities

Among their business skills, caterers have to be good with numbers. Just to figure out how much to charge their customers, caterers have to calculate a variety of costs, including ingredients, equipment, electricity and gas for cooking, transportation vehicle and fuel expenses, payments to kitchen and serving staffs, salaries for themselves, and **profit**. Profits are needed to help the business grow and to cover expenses such as supplies, advertising, and new kitchen equipment.

Some caterers start by working in restaurants, others take catering courses at culinary or **vocational schools**, and some people turn their cooking hobbies into catering jobs or businesses. All catering activity, however, must be licensed or certified by a board of health.

Organizational skills

Catering jobs can involve a lot of people and a lot of details. Food preparation must be orderly and efficient and must comply with health laws and other standards of cleanliness and safety. Caterers frequently find themselves preparing for several events at the same time. Keeping their kitchens running smoothly and making sure that the right food and the right staff are at the right events requires careful organization and attention to details.

Whether events are formal or casual, meeting the needs of customers' guests is every caterer's highest priority.

Communication skills

Whether selling their services to customers or giving instructions to kitchen or serving staff, caterers must be able to communicate clearly and effectively. They have to promote their services with confidence and pride and know how to motivate employees to work hard and maintain quality.

A day in the life of a caterer

Jackie Sullivan

Jackie runs her own catering business. She has always been a good cook, but before starting her business, she took a three-month catering course. She also studied the rules and regulations for being self-employed and the requirements for licensing by the board of health.

7:30 a.m.   I'm on my way to a local market to buy fresh fruit and vegetables for a retirement party this evening.

9:00 a.m.   I stop to visit a couple who wants me to cater a party for their anniversary, two months from now. They have just returned from living for several years in Hong Kong, so they would like me to prepare a Chinese menu. Their home is rather small for the forty guests they plan to invite, so I suggest a buffet with a Chinese theme. I take notes as we discuss specific menu items, and I check my appointment book to make sure I have reserved the date.

11:00 a.m.   Back at my home, I pack up tablecloths, glassware, plates, and cutlery for the retirement party, then head to the church kitchen I rent for preparing food. I run my business from my home, but I must prepare all foods in a licensed kitchen, which means that the kitchen meets strict health and safety standards for food preparation and has been inspected and approved by a licensing board. In my area, home kitchens cannot be licensed.

11:30 a.m.   My assistant, Sarah, arrives to help. The foods for tonight's event are easy-to-prepare meat and cheese trays, with several kinds of salads and desserts, but we're serving about one hundred people.

3:00 p.m.   Sarah and I load the food into my van and head off to the event, which is being held at a museum about twenty miles away.

6:00 p.m.   We have everything set up and ready when guests begin to arrive. Sarah and I spend the evening serving beverages and refilling empty food dishes.

7:00 p.m.   I take a moment to speak with the organizers of the event to make sure our work is satisfactory.

9:30 p.m.   The last guests are about to leave. After everyone is gone, it will take Sarah and me another hour or so to clean up and load the van.

Catering services are generally scheduled weeks, if not months, in advance, so caterers must have efficient and reliable systems for keeping track of their business commitments.

When preparing dishes for special events, only the freshest ingredients will do.

Chef

What is a chef?

Chefs are professional cooks who plan menus and select and prepare foods for restaurants, supper clubs, hotels, and other large establishments that serve meals to the public. *Chef* is a French word meaning "head" or "chief." Because France has long played a major role in the food and wine industries, many of the words used in professional cookery are French.

As the head of a large food service establishment, a chef has many responsibilities besides cooking.

A head chef is in charge of a restaurant or hotel's entire kitchen but may have an assistant, called a "sous (*soo*) chef." The kitchens in many large restaurants and hotels are divided into specialized departments. Each separate department, or area, is run by a *chef de partie* and is responsible for preparing a certain type of food. One area, for example, will prepare only meat or fish dishes, while another will make only desserts. Some kitchens also employ **apprentice** chefs. To gain the most experience, these trainees often work in several different food areas.

Dressed to Cook

For more than four hundred years, chefs have been easy to identify by the clothing they wear in the kitchen. The traditional chef's uniform, often called "chef's whites," includes a double-breasted jacket made of heavy white cotton, black or checkered pants, a white neckerchief that is knotted in front, and a tall, brimless, white hat, called a toque.

In smaller kitchens, one chef generally runs the entire operation and gives instructions to everyone working in the kitchen.

Family restaurants, cafeterias, and coffee shops usually serve less extravagant and less expensive meals than large restaurants and hotels serve. The people who prepare foods in these establishments are usually called cooks, rather than chefs. They may not have as much control over menus as chefs do and are generally more concerned with either larger quantities or fast service. In diners and fast-food and carryout restaurants, cooks are often known as short-order cooks.

The idea for chefs to wear different sized hats started in the mid-1800s. Chefs with more experience or **prestige** wore toques, while young cooks and apprentices wore white hats that looked like caps.

Main responsibilities of a chef

A chef's rank is what typically determines his or her responsibilities in the kitchen. The head chef in a large kitchen actually doesn't do very much cooking. A head chef's main responsibilities usually include:

- planning menus, making sure there are plenty of choices for diners with varying tastes or particular food preferences or restrictions. A chef should, for example, consider vegetarians, who do not eat meat, and vegans, who eat neither meat nor dairy products. They may also have Muslim or Jewish customers, who do not eat pork; Hindu customers, who eat no beef; or **diabetics**, who must control sugars.

When buying ingredients, the best chefs select only the freshest foods, such as live lobsters.

Good Points and Bad Points

"I love working with food. I especially enjoy being creative and experimenting with new dishes. And the atmosphere in the kitchen is exciting. At times, it's hectic, but that's part of the fun."

"The work can be physically exhausting. Although I have time off in the afternoon, it doesn't make up for working until late at night."

- creating distinctive dishes, defining preparation and cooking instructions, and selecting ingredients
- researching with various suppliers the prices, quality, and availability of food ingredients and kitchen equipment and making sure that orders are placed and received on time
- calculating the costs of producing dishes offered on the menu and setting menu prices to make sure the restaurant makes a **profit**. Chefs also need to be sure that the menu selections can be prepared within reasonable amounts of time. Customers will not usually put up with long delays.
- running the kitchen, which includes overall coordination of the staff as well as making sure that foods are prepared correctly and taste good. Particularly in fine restaurants, chefs must be as concerned with presentation, or the look and arrangement of food when it is served, as they are with taste.
- maintaining high standards of cleanliness and safety. Chefs must see to it that their kitchens, including all equipment, utensils, and workers, are clean and **sanitary** and that foods are stored properly and at the right temperatures.

In any restaurant kitchen, pots, pans, and all other utensils used for cooking or serving foods must be kept very clean.

Main qualifications of a chef

Cooking experience

A chef needs to be an excellent and creative cook, with sharp senses of taste and smell, who is fascinated with foods and ways to serve foods. Restaurant customers are always looking to try new foods and different food combinations, and it is the chef's job to provide them.

Leadership skills

The overall quality of a restaurant depends on the way a chef manages his or her staff. Chefs have to be able to give instructions to food preparation staff and many other kinds of workers and make sure the instructions are carried out. Chefs also have to be able to motivate workers to do their jobs well.

Trainees sharpen their **culinary** skills in restaurant kitchens, working, hands-on, under the supervision of one or more experienced chefs.

Organizational skills

Whether supervising a large staff or preparing several different dishes at the same time, a chef has to be able to work efficiently and know how to plan ahead. Even in the best-organized kitchens, however, foods burn, dishes break, and tempers flare. A chef must be able to maintain control and deal with problems of all kinds.

Math skills

Restaurants are businesses, and running them means working with numbers. Chefs must be able to calculate everything from ingredient quantities to menu prices.

Customers expect the food in a restaurant to look appetizing and be served promptly.

Communication skills

Chefs have to be able to communicate well, especially verbally. A kitchen staff needs clear, detailed instructions on a daily basis. Chefs may also have to communicate with restaurant owners, managers, servers, or customers, as well as with food suppliers and equipment companies. Writing skills can be helpful, too, although, for most chefs, the main form of communication is verbal.

A day in the life of a chef

Suzie Rosco

Suzie is an apprentice chef at a very busy restaurant. In addition to her on-the-job training, she attends classes at a local cooking school.

10:00 a.m.   The chefs here work a split shift, covering both lunch and dinner, so 10:00 a.m. seems early to me. The staff starts each day by making sure that everything in the kitchen is cleaned up and in place. Then the head chef briefs us on menu changes and any special food preparation details.

10:30 a.m.   I prepare vegetables for the lunchtime **clientele**, peeling potatoes and carrots and washing and chopping salad ingredients. The lunch menu is normally lighter in **fare** than the dinner menu. Lunch customers usually have less time to eat so they often order just one **course** and a beverage.

11:30 a.m.   The head chef, who is also the owner of the restaurant, gives me some tips on pastry making. I take notes, then get to work filling the pastry cases. One good thing about being a trainee is having a chance to try my hand at almost every job in the kitchen.

12:00 p.m.   Lunch traffic is heavy. I help fill orders by carrying plates to the various food preparation areas and checking to make sure the orders are correct and complete.

3:00 p.m.   The last of the lunch customers are gone, and the kitchen is ready for the dinner shift. I leave work between shifts and usually spend this time preparing for the classes I attend two days a week.

6:00 p.m. I'm back at the restaurant, making sauces and preparing vegetables. We have a few customers already, but the dinner rush won't start for another hour or so.

9:00 p.m. Dinner orders have been nonstop for two hours but are now beginning to slow down. I finally have a chance to sit and rest my feet for few minutes. I'll soon have to start cleaning up the kitchen.

10:00 p.m. I'm done for the day.

Chefs run kitchens in many different places. This chef prepares meals on a cruise ship.

Pastry making is an essential part of training for many chefs.

Cookbook Writer

What is a cookbook writer?

Cookbook writers, who are also known as food writers, create, test, and write recipes and other cooking- and food-related materials, such as articles and columns for books, magazines, newspapers, and even the Internet.

Writing cookbooks and food articles is a field a person usually gets into after gaining professional or practical cooking and food preparation experience some other way. Many food writers have worked as caterers or have run their own restaurants. Some are known for a certain type or style of cooking, such as vegetarian dishes or meals made in slow cookers. Others are specialists in particular kinds of foods, such as fish, wild **game**, cheese, or chocolate. Some focus on foods and cooking from other parts of the world, such as India or the Mediterranean.

Most cookbooks, today, are more than just collections of recipes. Their writers make them enjoyable to read, and plenty of mouth-watering photos make them a pleasure to look at.

Many cookbooks feature foods from faraway places, giving adventurous cooks a chance to offer exotic **fare** at any meal.

America's First Lady of Cooking

In 1921, a Minnesota milling company began sending out "personally" signed responses to the thousands of baking questions they received each year. Using the last name of a retired executive and the handwriting of a company secretary, the Washburn Crosby Company (now General Mills) introduced cooking **icon** "Betty Crocker."

Cookbook writers often inform readers about nutrition, food science, travel, and other topics. Many cookbooks also include personal accounts of writers' experiences, so that readers come to feel as if they actually know the authors. The photos, too, often go beyond just food to include landscapes from featured locales, along with descriptions of local history, culture, and folklore. Some cookbooks are written to coordinate with TV cooking series or to accompany kitchen appliances available for purchase.

A good cookbook often becomes one of the most important pieces of equipment in a kitchen.

Food writers for newspapers and magazines are often trained journalists who developed an interest in food and started writing about it. Some are **food critics**.

Main responsibilities of a cookbook writer

Famous cooks and chefs are often asked by publishers to write cookbooks or food articles. Cooks and writers who are not so well-known usually contact publishers with their ideas and try to interest one or more publishers in hiring them or contracting with them. Most food writers for **periodicals** have **contracts** to write articles or columns for a set fee and a fixed period of time. In writing for any kind of publication, however, the basic tasks are much the same.

A good cookbook writer tests each and every recipe.

- Research to find new recipes and new ways to prepare foods usually includes reading existing cookbooks, visiting restaurants, and traveling to particular regions or countries to find out what people eat and how they prepare their foods.

Good Points and Bad Points

"I love writing, and I love cooking, so I'm very lucky to have a job that involves both. I also love to travel, and I often plan trips around ideas for books. I enjoy wandering through food markets in exotic places and eating at all kinds of restaurants."

"Even the greatest ideas for cookbooks or food articles can be hard to sell to publishers and periodicals. Selling **freelance** work can take a lot of time, and living without a steady income is often difficult."

- Recipes must be created or adapted, then tested and modified, to meet publication requirements. Modifying a recipe might mean simplifying cooking instructions; replacing certain ingredients, perhaps because they are too expensive or difficult to find; or adjusting the amounts of ingredients, so the recipe serves a certain number of people.

- Producing the content of a book or article involves more than just writing it. The order of information is important, too. The structure of the work must be interesting and easy to follow.

- Photos, artwork, and other design elements require most writers to work closely with food photographers, and graphic artists and designers. Writers often take as much interest as designers in making sure that the **visuals** associated with a book or article are clear, appropriate, and attractive.

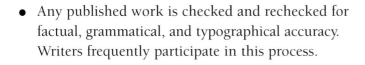

After all of the planning, research, and recipe testing, a cookbook author has a lot of writing to do.

- Any published work is checked and rechecked for factual, grammatical, and typographical accuracy. Writers frequently participate in this process.

- By doing publicity interviews and making other personal appearances, writers help sell their work.

Main qualifications of a cookbook writer

A fascination for foods

To be able to write authoritatively about foods and food preparation, cookbook writers need to know a lot about foods, from their histories to their nutritional contents. Because cookbook writers spend most of their working lives thinking about foods, learning about foods, talking about foods, and writing about foods, they must have a true fascination for foods.

When the author of a cookbook is famous, like the Duchess of York, the book is likely to be a big seller.

Cooking skills

Cookbook writers must be good cooks. They have to be able to write recipes and prepare them successfully before they can give cooking instructions to others. Knowledge of food preparation methods and kitchen equipment is important, too.

Research skills

Famous cookbook writers often hire research assistants to come up with new angles, recipes, ideas, and information for cookbooks and food-related articles. Most writers, however, do the majority of this research themselves.

Writing ability

Producing cookbooks and food articles that are both interesting and informative calls for a special combination of writing talents.

Besides looking delicious, photographs for cookbooks must be carefully selected to complement the recipes they illustrate.

Technical writing skills help in composing instructions that are clear, straightforward, and easy to follow. Creative writing skills keep main text, **sidebars**, and **fillers** lively, interesting, and fun to read.

fact file

Some cooking enthusiasts simply have a cookbook idea and are lucky enough to find a publisher. Other cookbook authors are trained cooks, chefs, or caterers who can also write. Sometimes, professional writers and cooks **collaborate**.

Teamwork

Even cookbook authors who do all of the research and writing themselves are part of a team and must be able to work effectively with all other members of the team, including designers, editors, photographers, and marketing and publicity professionals.

A day in the life of a cookbook writer

Shara Madi

Shara grew up in Turkey, where her mother taught her how to cook. She has always loved cooking and has written several cookbooks that feature Eastern European dishes.

6:30 a.m. I work from an office in my home. I started work very early this morning because I'm supposed to have a first **draft** of the manuscript for my new cookbook ready to send to my publisher tomorrow.

9:00 a.m. I stop working to take my daughter to school. I've managed to get a lot done already, and I'm pleased that telephone calls haven't disturbed me.

11:00 a.m. I spoke too soon about the phone. I've been on it now for the past hour, talking to my editor. He wants to arrange a meeting with a designer so we can decide how the book should look. He also wants me to send him any family photos I have that show our life in Turkey. He has a lot of good ideas, but I need to get back to work.

12:00 p.m. The phone rings again! This call is from a TV station that wants to use my recipes on a cooking program. The program sounds exciting, so I make an appointment to meet with the station manager.

A lot of research goes into writing a good cookbook.

Bookstores carry an interesting variety of cookbooks these days.

12:30 p.m.   I'm off the phone and back at my computer, when I notice an E-mail from the editor of a magazine I write for. He wants me to check the accuracy of a fact in a nutrition article I submitted last week. He needs my verification right away, so I have to put off working on the cookbook a little longer.

1:30 p.m.   At last, I'm ready to work on the manuscript again. I call my husband at his office and ask him to pick up our daughter from school so I can make up for lost time on the cookbook.

6:30 p.m.   I'll be working until very late tonight, so my husband has prepared dinner and is taking care of our daughter. Publishing deadlines are sometimes hard on the whole family.

Dietitian

What is a dietitian?

Dietitians study foods and nutrition, then use their knowledge to teach people how to eat properly and how to plan diets and nutrition programs that help prevent and treat illnesses. Some dietitians, especially those who work in hospitals, schools, and other large institutions, may also supervise meal preparation.

In recent years, dietitians, other health care providers, and health research organizations have all been trying to make people more aware of the harmful effects of certain eating habits for people of all ages. Poor diet can mean either eating too many high-fat foods, salty

Dietitians often design programs that can help parents teach their children to make healthy food choices.

A Burger King

A tiny Connecticut sandwich shop, built in 1895, may be the place where hamburgers were born. Its founder, Louis Lassen, didn't want to waste any leftover beef from the steak sandwiches he sold to local factory workers at his lunch wagon, so he ground up the meat, grilled it, and served it between two slices of white bread. The little diner, called Louis Lunch, still makes hamburgers this way today.

snacks and sugary desserts, or not eating enough fresh fruits, vegetables, and whole grains. Poor eating habits are one of the main reasons why so many people today, including children, are overweight. Poor diets are also a major cause of life-threatening health conditions, including cancer, heart disease, and **diabetes**.

Dietitians work in a variety of ways and a variety of places. Some are self-employed in **private practices** for nutritional counseling and consulting, while others work in hospitals or nursing homes, helping patients who need dietary advice and assistance to cope with specific health problems. **Diabetics**, for example, need to learn how to control their blood sugar levels by knowing what and when to eat. People with heart problems need help avoiding fatty foods and eating more vegetables and fruits. People with allergies to dairy, wheat, and other foods, need to be introduced to safe and healthful alternatives.

One of the goals of dietitians is to steer people away from foods with too much fat, salt, and sugar.

Main responsibilities of a dietitian

Most of the responsibilities of dietitians fall into one of the following categories.

Education and research

- participating in ongoing research in the fields of food science and nutrition, conducted primarily at universities, hospitals, and medical laboratories
- developing instructional programs and literature for schools, community health centers, businesses, organizations, groups, and individuals to help promote healthy food choices and eating habits
- analyzing foods to determine the nutritional values that appear on product labels and in recipes
- consulting with food manufacturers to help improve the quality of foods and ingredients and to recommend the cleanest and safest processing methods

Helping children learn to choose nutritious foods is one of the best ways to keep them healthy.

Good Points and Bad Points

"As more becomes known about the effects that different foods have on the human body, my job becomes increasingly interesting."

"Although I enjoy my work, I find it depressing to see the amount of junk food children are eating, both at meals and for snacks."

Planning and counseling

- determining the specific needs of medical patients and other individuals seeking nutritional guidance
- designing special diets and eating plans for particular medical conditions as well as general health needs
- assisting individuals in adapting to dietary changes
- evaluating the results of nutritional programs and making changes and adjustments as needed
- working with doctors and other health care providers in coordinating treatments for physical, emotional, behavioral, and nutritional problems

Management

- overseeing large-scale food preparation in schools, hospitals, prisons, corporate cafeterias, and other institutions and facilities
- enforcing health and safety laws and regulations related to food service operations
- serving as nutritional consultants to caterers, sports teams, and other food- or nutrition-related businesses

Main qualifications of a dietitian

Science knowledge

A dietitian works in a science-based profession and needs a strong science background. Biology, chemistry, and physiology are essential, along with other sciences related to health, foods, and nutrition. Specialized branches of science, such as biochemistry and microbiology are also recommended.

Research skills

Even dietitians in positions that are not directly involved with research need to understand research and scientific methods and know how to interpret results and reports. Almost daily reports delivering new or revised information on how foods affect the human body make keeping up with the latest developments essential for every dietitian.

Communication skills

Explaining scientific and medical information in a simple way is a big part of most dietitians' jobs. To communicate effectively with patients and clients, many of whom are children or aging adults, dietitians have to know how to change complex technical language into everyday words and make difficult concepts easy to understand. When teaching classes, conducting **seminars**, or speaking with individuals or groups in any setting, dietitians must make sure that information is not only understandable but also interesting and lively.

To help people succeed in correcting poor eating habits, dietitians try to make nutrition information easy to understand and eating plans easy to follow.

Meeting with shoppers right at the supermarket is one of the ways a dietitian can teach people the difference between healthy and unhealthy food products.

fact file

A dietitian must have earned a bachelor's degree in **dietetics**, nutrition, or a closely related field. Supervised practice in an **accredited internship** program is also needed. For most jobs, dietitians must be licensed, or registered, and research positions may require an advanced degree.

Tact and patience

Most people have trouble changing their eating habits, and dietitians need to help without making anyone feel guilty or ashamed. People with medical problems or eating disorders are often particularly depressed or easily upset. Dietitians need to show concern and respect for these patients and help them set specific, realistic goals for making behavioral changes. Dietitians must remember, too, that changes do not happen overnight. Patients often fall back into old habits for a while, so progress can take a long time.

A day in the life of a dietitian

George Davis

George has a bachelor's degree in dietetics and a master's degree in clinical nutrition. He has been working as a hospital dietitian for fourteen years.

8:45 a.m. I check my E-mail messages and today's schedule.

9:00 a.m. The first thing on my schedule is a meeting with the **pediatric** medical team to discuss treatment plans for children with food allergies.

10:30 a.m. I meet with the catering manager to talk over menus for inpatients. Preparing these menus is a difficult job. All meals have to meet specific nutritional standards, and we have to provide alternatives for people with special dietary needs. The food has to be healthy and look attractive, and we have to do it all on a very tight budget.

12:00 p.m. It's lunchtime, but I have some phone calls, letters, and other administrative work that has to be done first.

1:45 p.m. Now, I'm really hungry. I head to the cafeteria for a sandwich.

2:30 p.m. I'm scheduled for after-noon appointments in the outpatient clinic. My first appointment is with the parents of an overweight six-year-old. We talk about making changes to improve the whole family's

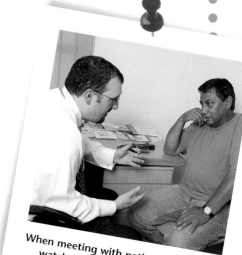

When meeting with patients, dietitians watch for signs of problems that could lead to serious illnesses.

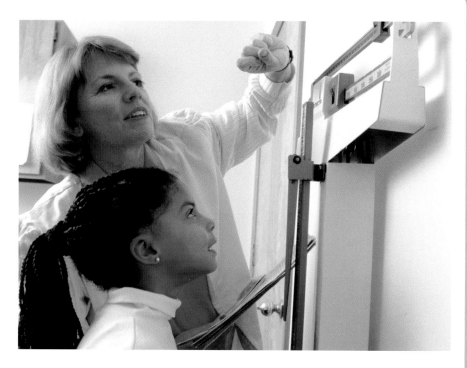

As children grow, checking their weight on a regular basis is important. Unusual weight gain or loss can be a sign of illness, but, more often, it is the result of poor eating habits. Dietitians are often consulted to help with children's weight problems.

diet and schedule a follow-up appointment for a month from now.

3:30 p.m. I talk to a mother with an underweight toddler. The woman is very slim. She is obviously weight conscious and says she visits the gym regularly. She tells me that her daughter doesn't have a big appetite. I give her some specific food and menu suggestions and ask that she bring her daughter back in two weeks.

4:30 p.m. Concerned about the toddler's health, I phone her pediatrician to find out more about the child's medical history.

5:00 p.m. I leave the hospital, but my day isn't over yet. I have to talk about healthy eating habits to a group of people recovering from heart attacks.

Food Photographer

Food photographers take pictures of all kinds of foods for use in cookbooks, magazines, newspapers, and advertisements. Some food photographers work as staff members for publishing companies, but most work **freelance**. Many start their careers by assisting established photographers.

Food photography takes a lot of planning, and getting a good food shot is not easy. Food does not look very appetizing for very long. Most food photography takes place in a studio rather than on location. The dishes to be photographed are prepared and arranged in attractive settings by **food stylists**. These cooking professionals specialize in making foods look good for the camera.

A good food photograph can actually make a person feel hungry!

The arrival of **digital** technology has changed the work of food photographers in recent years. Digital cameras have made the shooting process easier because no actual film is involved, which means no need to reload cameras. A lot of the work is now done after the photos have been taken. With today's specialized software programs, photographers can touch up, correct, and manipulate images on computers, instead of having to reshoot them.

Double Take

Photographing foods is tricky, especially keeping the foods looking fresh and appetizing while food stylists are arranging and **garnishing** and photographers are setting lights. Food stylists have been known to use tricks, such as substituting mashed potatoes for ice cream, to replace fragile foods with sturdier "look-alikes," but most foods are real. They are just prepared twice! The first foods are stand-ins for setting up the shot. The second foods are final. The real trick is in the timing.

When images are loaded onto a computer, they can be combined in creative and interesting ways. A food shot taken in a studio, for example, can be combined with a photo of a picnic on a mountainside, making the food look as if it were part of the picnic. Using computers, photographers can also create a variety of special effects. A splash shot, for example, captures the moment an object, such as an ice cube, hits some kind of liquid in a tumbler and causes a splash.

Photographers meet with their clients before **photo shoots** to decide the kinds of photographic effects the clients might want.

In the past, if a photo did not turn out absolutely right, it would need to be shot again. Now photos can be **retouched** on a computer to remove imperfections, such as a wilting lettuce leaf or a smear of sauce on the edge of a plate.

Main responsibilities of a food photographer

The key to a successful photo shoot is planning.
At this stage, clients or their representatives, such as marketing directors or graphic designers, work with food photographers and food stylists to decide:

- the number and types of shots that are needed
- the composition of each shot, or how each shot should look
- the **props** that will be used
- the type of lighting required

Although the client or company representative will usually have a say in the number and types of photos needed for a shoot, the photographer makes all of the technical decisions, such as what kind of camera equipment to use and how to set lighting to achieve the best effects.

A successful food photographer knows how to use a variety of photographic equipment.

Good Points and Bad Points

"The variety of work is exciting. No two workdays are the same."

"Food photography is often seen as the poor, unglamorous relative of fashion photography."

At a photo shoot, a photographer's assistant is often the person who looks after and arranges props.

Preparation for some photo shoots can take several hours. While chefs or food stylists prepare and arrange the food, photographers set up lighting and backgrounds. The photo shoot, however, is actually a fairly small part of most food photographers' jobs. Other responsibilities include:

- promoting the business and finding clients
- writing estimates and negotiating fees
- ordering supplies
- hiring assistants
- running the business, including collecting payments, bookkeeping, taxes, and **copyright registration**

Main qualifications of a food photographer

Technical skills

The ability to use cameras and many other kinds of photographic equipment with confidence is an essential requirement for a career in food photography. Graphic designers and food stylists, as well as clients, depend on photographers for technical advice. But technical skills alone are not enough to be a successful food photographer.

Artistic ability

Making food photographs look elegant, eye-catching, and good enough to eat requires creative ideas and artistic vision, so food photographers need to know how to combine artistic skills with their technical expertise. They must, for example, know how to use light creatively and, at the same time, know how to achieve the desired effects with either natural light or special lighting equipment.

Computer skills

Digital photography is replacing film photography to the extent that traditional cameras may, one day, be replaced entirely by digital equipment. Digital technology has given photographers exciting new opportunities. In using digital cameras, however, food photographers must also know how to use the computer programs and software designed to make the most of digital images.

Adding final touches to food before shooting the photo is an example of the photographer's artistic skills.

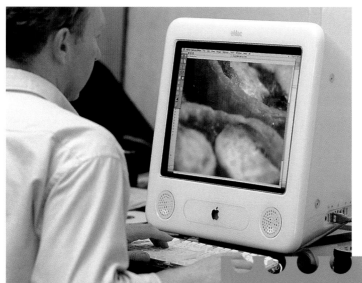

Computers can be used to alter digital photos in many ways, from touching up tiny imperfections or making simple color corrections to combining several images or making dramatic modifications.

fact file

Most photographers have some type of formal education or training in photography. Many also have taken art courses or have some kind of **culinary** training. One of the best ways to get started in a career as a food photographer is by working as an assistant to an established, professional food photographer.

Patience

Food photographs can take many hours of planning and preparation. A lot of time and effort goes into meeting with clients, selling ideas, preparing for shoots, and achieving successful results.

Teamwork

A food photographer must be willing and able to work as part of a team, with chefs, food stylists, graphic designers, and photographic assistants.

Determination

Professional photography is often seen as a glamorous career, but it is fiercely competitive work, and finding jobs can be tough. Photographers must be confident in selling their work and able to cope with rejection.

Lee Hacker

Lee completed a professional photography course, then did some work as a fashion photographer before specializing in food photography.

8:30 a.m. I spend some time doing bookkeeping and sending out **invoices** to collect money clients owe me. Because I'm self-employed, I have to allow time for paperwork.

10:00 a.m. I telephone a few people who might be able to give me some work in the future. Making and keeping up with contacts is a good way to promote business and find new clients.

10:30 a.m. I meet with a well-known and highly respected food photographer. I started my own career in food photography by working as his assistant, and I've learned a lot from him. He invites me to work with him, again, on a couple of new projects. Both of them sound exciting, and one of them fits very well into my schedule. Unfortunately, I have to pass on the other one.

When the photographer does a good job, the food looks too good to resist.

12:15 p.m.   I start an hour-long drive to a food production company that needs a photographer to take some advertising shots.

1:30 p.m.   The company's marketing manager explains the advertising campaign to me and tells me what kinds of photos she wants to include. I show her my **portfolio** and hope she's impressed.

4:30 p.m.   Back home, I check my phone messages. A contact has called, asking me to meet with him at 8:00 p.m. I have to get up at 6:00 a.m. tomorrow for a shoot that will last about twelve hours, but this contact said there's a big job coming up, and I can't afford to miss a chance at the work. I call him back and agree to meet.

5:00 p.m.   The marketing manager I met with earlier calls to say I've got the job. We discuss the fee and schedule the shoot for two weeks from now.

With digital cameras, food photographers can shoot as many images as they like without having to reload film.

Food Technologist

What is a food technologist?

Food technologists are scientists dedicated to the study, development, and discovery of foods. They work for research organizations, food processing companies, and food suppliers, making sure that the foods people eat taste good and meet lifestyle and dietary needs as well as established standards for quality, nutrition, and safety.

The variety of canned and packaged foods available today is enormous.

Over the last fifty years, much has changed in the way of meal preparation. Before the 1960s, most married women did not have jobs outside the home. They shopped for fresh meats and vegetables several times a week and cooked meals for their families every day. Many baked breads, cakes, pies, and cookies, from scratch, on a weekly basis.

Today, most women have jobs in the workforce and spend a lot less time than their grandmothers did buying food and preparing meals. People today buy many **convenience foods**.

Empire of Ice

People have been preserving foods by freezing them for several centuries, but Clarence Birdseye created a **commercial** empire of frozen foods. Living in Labrador, in 1916, Birdseye noticed that foods frozen in that region's Arctic climate in winter tasted better than foods frozen at warmer times of the year. He realized that the faster the freezing process, the less chance for ice crystals to damage the food. Birdseye used this knowledge to invent a revolutionary food-freezing process.

Most households now have refrigerators and freezers stocked with a variety of foods and meals that just have to be warmed in an oven, heated on a stove, or microwaved before they can be eaten.

Along with convenience, however, have come reports of food poisoning and other fears related to the quality of processed foods. Food technologists have been instrumental in setting, maintaining, and monitoring standards of health and safety to relieve these kinds of concerns.

Making sure that food processing complies with health and safety standards is often the job of a food technologist.

Main responsibilities of a food technologist

Many food technologists work in research laboratories or test kitchens, developing new food products and improving existing ones. Aspects of food production that benefit from this research include:

- lengthening the shelf life of food products (in other words, keeping foods fresh and fit to eat for longer periods of time)
- simplifying cooking and serving methods (For people with busy lives, the easier it is to heat foods and put them on the table, the more popular those foods will be.)
- enhancing the flavors of foods (Whether foods are canned, frozen, or ready to eat, people want them to taste as if they were freshly made that day.)

Before a new food product is sold to the public, technologists run many tests on small amounts to find and correct any problems.

Good Points and Bad Points

"There isn't much I don't like about my job. I enjoy working in a laboratory, and the work I do is interesting and varied."

"The level of concentration needed to do my job can sometimes be very stressful. I must constantly keep in mind that the slightest slip, such as a mistake reading the results of an experiment, can cause great harm."

Tastes and food preferences change frequently. One year, Thai food may be popular; the next year, Italian. With improvements in transportation for both travel and shipping, people now enjoy a far greater variety of foods than they did fifty years ago, including foods from all over the world. Food technologists play important roles in:

- making the foods people enjoy readily available
- ensuring that foods produced in factories meet set standards for size, color, and taste
- monitoring food **imports** to confirm their compliance with government standards for health and safety

Strict laws dictate how foods sold to the public must be produced, stored, and transported. It is the job of food technologists to develop systems and procedures for making sure the laws and regulations are followed.

Advancements in technology over the past ten to fifteen years have dramatically changed the way food is processed. At some jobs, technologists seem more like mechanics.

Main qualifications of a food technologist

Science and mathematics background

Food technologists need to have high-level knowledge in a variety of sciences, especially biology, chemistry, and physics, to understand the nature of foods, the substances they contain, the ways foods change, and why. They also need to be competent in mathematics, including calculus, to deal with the numerical calculations and statistical techniques that are involved in food research.

Technologists look at food from a mainly scientific point of view. These technologists are taking a sample of cheese to determine its nutritional value for labeling purposes.

Teamwork

Although some of the responsibilities of food technologists, especially many research-related tasks, require working independently, food technologists must also be able to work as part of a team. Most food technologists perform both research and nonresearch tasks that involve close contact with other individuals or groups, including:

- other technologists, who may be doing similar or related research
- research chefs, who create new recipes and food combinations
- dietitians, who are interested in the nutritional value and quality of foods

- **economists**, who figure out the cost of producing foods and suggest the prices at which foods should be sold
- **manufacturers and processors**, who produce foods in large quantities to be sold to consumers

This food technologist is testing **cacao** for use in chocolate production.

Communication skills

An important part of a food technologist's job is explaining his or her findings to others, both verbally and in writing. The communication must be clear and concise, and technical language must be simplified.

Computer skills

Food technologists use computers for many tasks, especially collecting and storing information, analyzing data, producing reports, and giving presentations.

Business skills

The tasks performed by food technologists are usually parts of large projects. As project managers, technologists need to be able to make decisions, solve problems, organize and prioritize tasks, and supervise other workers.

fact file

A food technologist must have a college degree, and research jobs usually require an advanced degree. Degrees are typically in agricultural or food science, and course work usually includes food chemistry, analysis, microbiology, and processing.

Harry Chung

Harry is a trainee food technician at a research facility that does testing and problem-solving for large food preparation and manufacturing companies. Harry's company offers training courses attended by food technologists from all over the world.

9:00 a.m. I arrive at the lab, which is where I spend most of my workday. I'm starting about an hour later than usual, today, but the company has **flextime**.

9:30 a.m. I'm set up this morning for testing various food ingredients to determine their nutritional values. Verifying these values is important for making sure that product labels contain accurate information.

11:30 a.m. I meet with my manager to talk over the progress I'm making and to review my findings. When it comes to quality research, our company has an international reputation to maintain.

1:30 p.m. On my way back to the lab, I stop at the cafeteria for some lunch. Working with food all day rarely spoils my appetite.

2:15 p.m. I'm back in the lab, checking some final data for a project report that I have to complete today.

Food technologists generally store test results in computer files and databases.

The project involved testing various preparation methods for a new line of convenience foods. My report must contain detailed testing procedures and results, as well as my recommendations for the instructions that will appear on the packaging. The manufacturer needs my report to complete package designs and start production.

6:00 p.m. The report took me longer to write than I had planned. I have to work quickly now to prepare for a presentation I'm making this evening to a golfers' organization. My career goal is to specialize in nutrition and dietary advice that can help improve performance in specific sports.

In today's fast-paced world, frozen dinners that can be heated in microwave ovens are extremely popular. Over the years, food technologists have helped many food manufacturers improve the variety and nutritional value of these convenience foods.

Restaurant Manager

What is a restaurant manager?

Restaurant managers direct the daily operations of businesses that serve food and beverages. They are the links between the staff in restaurant kitchens who prepare the food, the staff in dining areas who serve the food, and the customers who eat the food. In other words, restaurant managers are people in charge of restaurants. They make sure that the food is good, the customers are happy, the staff are doing their jobs properly, and the business is making money.

Restaurants that look inviting may attract customers, but it is the quality of a restaurant's food and service that keeps customers coming back.

Fast-Food McManagers

In 1948, Richard and Maurice McDonald opened a restaurant in San Bernadino, California. They offered fifteen-cent hamburgers, and they served them *fast*! Ray Kroc had never seen so many hamburgers served so fast. In 1955, Kroc started the first McDonald's fast-food franchise. Today, there are some thirty thousand McDonald's restaurants — worldwide!

Some restaurants belong to a group, or chain, of dozens, hundreds, or even thousands of outlets or **franchises**. All the restaurants in a chain will often look similar. They may all be decorated the same way and may feature the same menu items. The administrative staff at a group's headquarters set policies and make decisions for all of the group's restaurants, and it is the job of each restaurant's manager to see that group policies are followed and instructions are carried out.

The manager is often the first to greet customers in a restaurant. Making them feel welcome is a good first step to ensuring that customers enjoy their meals.

Independent restaurants are not parts of chains. They develop foods, menus, and styles of **decor** that are all their own. At an independent restaurant, the manager is typically responsible for establishing policies and making business plans and decisions, as well as putting policies, plans, and decisions into practice. In some cases, the manager is also the owner of the restaurant.

Main responsibilities of a restaurant manager

A restaurant manager is responsible for many areas of activity in the restaurant, from hiring staff and greeting customers to purchasing supplies and making bank deposits.

In dealing with customers, a restaurant manager makes sure that:

- the restaurant is clean and looks inviting
- customers are greeted when they arrive and are seated as quickly as possible
- food orders are taken promptly and served correctly
- complaints are dealt with politely

Staff-related responsibilities include:

- recruiting, interviewing, and hiring
- organizing training sessions
- preparing work schedules
- dealing with discipline problems

Making sure that staff are properly trained, suitably dressed, and polite to customers is an important part of a restaurant manager's job.

Good Points and Bad Points

"Working at the front of the restaurant gives me a chance to meet and talk to many interesting people. I get a lot of satisfaction from making sure they are comfortable and giving them an opportunity to relax and enjoy a fine meal."

"The hours are long. I work most evenings and weekends, so I don't have much opportunity for a social life outside the restaurant."

Most restaurant managers take care of a variety of business and money matters, which can include any of the following tasks.

- calculating the costs of, and paying bills for, both food and non-food supplies
- setting the prices of meals and other menu items
- handling the money taken in from customers and checking to see that it **tallies** with the receipts for meals served
- making sure that the money taken in each day is secured in a safe or vault or deposited in a bank account

Managers of independent restaurants are often expected to develop the business and attract customers, which can involve:

- sponsoring events, such as wine tastings or holiday theme parties
- planning distinctive menus for special events and parties
- thinking up and promoting discount rates and offers, such as party packages, contests, and coupons in newspapers and magazines
- overseeing the production of advertisements to run in selected publications

Frequently, restaurant managers are also involved in coordinating redecoration projects and replacing furniture and equipment.

Although a lot of the actual kitchen responsibilities are left to chefs, many restaurant managers are still very involved in procedures and decisions related to menus, food preparation, staff, and equipment.

Main qualifications of a restaurant manager

Business knowledge
Restaurant managers need to know how businesses operate, in general, and should have first-hand work experience in a restaurant or some other food service business. The kinds of business skills typically used in restaurants include administration, finance and accounting (mathematics), and sales and marketing.

Communication and leadership skills
Whether they are dealing with employees, suppliers, or customers, restaurant managers spend most of their time working with other people. Because they must interact successfully with so many different groups of people, having strong communication skills, verbal and written, is very important. They also have to be good leaders, who know how to use their communication skills to direct and motivate employees, negotiate with suppliers, and persuade customers.

A restaurant manager usually is in charge of the restaurant's budget, which includes ordering equipment and supplies.

Stamina
Long work hours require restaurant managers to have a lot of staying power. Even in restaurants that close between mealtimes, managers often have to use that time for planning or paperwork. Other physical demands include having to do a lot of standing, lifting, bending, and walking during the course of a day.

Balancing cash and credit receipts at the end of the day is one of the reasons why a restaurant manager needs to have cash handling and bookkeeping experience.

fact file

Some restaurant managers are promoted to their positions based on work experience as a kitchen assistant or dining room employee. Others go through formal education or training programs. Some colleges offer two- or four-year degrees in restaurant management, and many large restaurant chains provide on-the-job training.

Problem-solving abilities
Equipment failures, double-booked **reservations**, and staff shortages are only a few of the problems restaurant managers face, and they are expected to resolve problems quickly, without upsetting or embarrassing anyone, especially customers. Even in the best-run restaurants, however, difficulties with customers arise. Most customers are polite, but on occasion, some can be rude or hostile. In these instances, restaurant managers must stay calm and composed but still maintain firm control of the situation. Managers who keep their tempers help customers keep theirs.

A day in the life of a restaurant manager

Jane Stokes

Jane owns and manages a restaurant she started with her best friend, who is a chef. The restaurant has been in business for four years. It is a small, but busy, operation, with only two kitchen assistants and two waitstaff for each shift, but Jane is hoping to expand in the near future.

9:30 a.m. I check that the restaurant has been cleaned to my satisfaction and make sure that tablecloths and napkins are back from the laundry. I discuss menu changes with Jack, my partner and our chef. He wants to introduce more fish dishes.

10:00 a.m. The early-shift staff arrive. They set tables and check reservations. I go into my office to pay bills and work on some publicity materials.

11:30 a.m. The restaurant sounds busy. I go to the dining room to greet customers and help take orders.

3:00 p.m. We close the restaurant between lunch and dinner, so the staff leave, and Jack and I meet with an architect about enlarging the restaurant.

3:45 p.m. A kitchen assistant calls to say that she's sick and can't work tonight. I contact one of the assistants from the early shift, who agrees to come back.

4:00 p.m. I go home to shower and change my clothes. A big part of my job is greeting customers, so my appearance is important.

5:00 p.m. I'm back at the restaurant. The evening shift started at 4:30 p.m. so I make sure that the staff have checked reservations and have the kitchen and dining room set up for dinner customers.

6:00 p.m. Business is quiet, so I do some bookkeeping.

7:30 p.m. A burst of activity brings me back to the dining room. I'm greeting customers nonstop and seating them as quickly as tables are available. A young couple arrives, insisting they have a reservation. When I can't find the reservation, they become very angry and start raising their voices. To calm them down, I apologize and offer them a discount on their dinners.

10:30 p.m. It's time to clean up and tally tonight's receipts. Then I can go home!

If customers are enjoying themselves, then the restaurant's manager is probably doing a good job.

At small restaurants, managers must be prepared to do any task, even waiting on tables themselves.

Glossary

accredited – approved or recognized as an authority or as meeting specific standards or requirements

apprentice – a person who is learning a job on the job, receiving training from a more experienced worker

buffet – a style of meal service in which prepared foods are set out for diners to choose from and help themselves

cacao – the seeds of a South American tree, from which cocoa and chocolate are made

chef de partie – the person in charge of a particular section or department in a restaurant kitchen

clientele – a group of clients, or customers

collaborate – to work with others in a cooperative way on a single task or project, usually with each worker contributing some kind of specialized knowledge or skills

commercial – having to do with commerce or mass marketing, which involves the large-scale buying and selling of goods

contract – a legal agreement that defines a business arrangement, exchanging goods or services for a specified amount of money during a specified time period

convenience foods – meals or separate food items that are already prepared, or partially prepared, when they are purchased or can be prepared or heated quickly and easily, especially by using a microwave oven

copyright registration – the process of officially claiming legal ownership of an artistic, musical, or literary work

course – a portion of a meal served separately from other parts of the meal, such as a salad (first course), served before a main dish (second course), served before a dessert (third course)

culinary – having to do with cooking or kitchens

decor – the arrangement, furnishings, and decorative and design elements of an interior space

diabetes – a disease (*diabetes mellitus*) that affects the body's ability to process carbohydrates such as sugar and starch

diabetics – people who have diabetes

dietetics – the study of foods, eating habits, and nutrition and how they relate to human health

digital – having to do with information and images recorded as numbers, or numerical digits, in an electronic device such as a computer

draft – an early version of written work, from which a final, more polished, product will be developed

economists – people who study the production and distribution of goods and services

fare – the kinds of dishes or menu items available for or served at meals

fillers – text or graphic additions used to fill space between or around main texts in books, magazines, or newspapers

flextime – a scheduling system that lets employees decide when, usually within a range of hours, they will start and end their workdays

food critics – people whose jobs are to judge the quality of foods prepared by others, especially in restaurants

food stylists – people who arrange foods in attractive ways for photographing

franchises – businesses that are owned individually but are authorized to use the name of and sell the goods and services developed by a founding organization

freelance – self-employed and free to work for more than one client

game – animals, such as deer, rabbits, pheasants, and grouse, that are traditionally hunted for food

garnishing – adding decorative, usually edible, touches, such as parsley sprigs or lemon wedges, to food dishes

icon – an honored person or object

imports – items brought in to a country, usually to be sold to local consumers

internship – a period of on-the-job training for a profession

invoices – itemized bills requesting payments for goods or services

pediatric – having to do with the health and medical treatment of children

periodicals – printed publications, such as magazines and newspapers, that are produced at specific time intervals

photo shoots – sessions during which photographs are taken

portfolio – a collection of art work or photographs used to display the artist's or photographer's skills to potential buyers or employers

prestige – fame or popularity

private practices – businesses in which people work for themselves, personally taking on all related risks and benefits

profit – the amount of financial gain after all expenses have been subtracted

props – short for "properties," which are objects added to create attractive or realistic arrangements for photographs

reservations – arrangements made in advance to hold objects or space for private or personal use at a later time

retouched – reworked or altered to improve appearance

sanitary – free of dirt and germs

seminars – study groups or scheduled meetings to discuss information on particular topics

sidebars – short stories or text related to and used to accompany main stories or articles in books or periodicals

tallies – adds up

venue – the place or location where a specific event will be or is being held

visuals – photographs, artwork, or graphic designs used to illustrate or decorate pages of text

vocational schools – educational institutions that focus on preparing students for careers in skilled trades

Further Information

This book does not cover all of the jobs in the food industry. Many jobs are not mentioned, including food manufacturer, waitstaff, and food stylist. This book does, however, give you an idea of what working in the food industry is like.

The food and catering industries offer many interesting career opportunities, working not only in restaurants but also in factories, schools, hospitals, and laboratories. Some workers in food-related professions advise people on healthy eating. There are food-related jobs in other fields, too, including advertising, photography, and journalism.

The only way to decide if working in the food industry is right for you is to find out what this kind of work involves. Read as much as you can about food-related careers and talk to people, especially people you know, who work in the food industry.

When you are in middle school or high school, a teacher or career counselor might be able to help you arrange some work experience in a certain career. For careers in the food industry, that experience could mean helping out in a school or hospital cafeteria or visiting a catering or restaurant kitchen or a nutrition clinic and watching what goes on and how the people who work there spend their time.

Books

Choosing a Career in Nutrition
Sue Hurwitz
(Rosen, 1999)

Cool Careers for Girls in Food
Ceel Pasternak and Linda Thornburg
(Impact, 1999)

Careers Without College: Food Service Manager
Kathryn A. Quinlan
(Capstone, 1999)

I Want to Be a Chef
Stephanie Maze
(Harcourt, 1999)

Web Sites

Agricultural and Food Scientist
www.bls.gov/k12/nature05.htm

CareerKids.com: Dietician
www.careerkids.com/careers/dietician.html

Interview with Iris Richardson, Food Photographer
www.cookingschools.com/interviews/iris-richardson/

Useful Addresses

Caterer

International Caterers Association
1200 17th Street NW
Washington, DC 20036
Tel: (888) 604-5844
www.icacater.org

Chef

Professional Chef's Association
1207 Hawkeye Court
Fort Collins, CO 80525
Tel: (970) 223-4004
www.professionalchef.com

The Culinary Institute of America
1946 Campus Drive
Hyde Park, NY 12538-1499
Tel: (845) 452-9600
www.ciachef.edu
www.ciakids.com/forkids/

Cookbook Writer

Association of Food Journalists
38309 Genessee Lake Road
Oconomowoc, WI 53066
Tel: (262) 965-3251
www.afjonline.com

Dietitian

American Dietetic Association
120 S. Riverside Plaza, Suite 2000
Chicago, IL 60606-6995
Tel: (800) 877-1600
www.eatright.org

Food Photographer

Professional Photographers of
America, Inc. (PPA) and Student
Photographic Society (SPS)
229 Peachtree Street NE, Suite 2200
Atlanta, GA 30303
Tel: (404) 522-8600 (800) 786-6277
SPS: (866) 886-5325
www.ppa.com
www.studentphoto.com

Food Technologist

Institute of Food Technologists
525 W. VanBuren, Suite 1000
Chicago, IL 60607
Tel: (312) 782-8424
www.ift.org/cms/?pid=1000411

Research Chefs Association
5775 Peachtree-Dunwoody Rd.
Bldg. G, Suite 500
Atlanta, GA 30342
Tel: (404) 252-3663
www.culinology.com

Restaurant Manager

National Restaurant Association (NRA)
1200 17th Street NW
Washington, DC 20036-3097
Tel: (202) 331-5900 (800) 424-5156
www.restaurant.org/careers/
www.nraef.org (NRA Educational
Foundation)

Index